CARBON

A TRUE BOOK®
by
Salvatore Tocci

Children's Press®
A Division of Scholastic Inc.

New York Toronto London Auckland Sydney
Mexico City New Delhi Hong Kong
Danbury, Connecticut

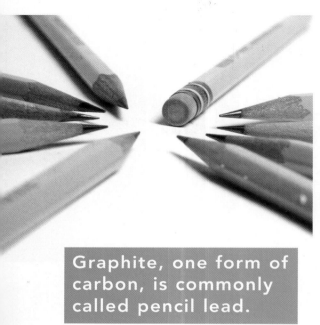

Graphite, one form of carbon, is commonly called pencil lead.

Reading Consultant
Julia McKenzie Munemo, EdM
New York, New York

Content Consultant
John A. Benner
Austin, Texas

The photo on the cover shows coal burning. The photo on the title page shows a graphite crystal.

The author and the publisher are not responsible for injuries or accidents that occur during or from any experiments. Experiments should be conducted in the presence of or with the help of an adult. Any instructions of the experiments that require the use of sharp, hot, or other unsafe items should be conducted by or with the help of an adult.

Library of Congress Cataloging-in-Publication Data

Tocci, Salvatore.
Carbon / by Salvatore Tocci.
    p. cm. — (A true book)
    Includes index.
    Contents: Can opposites be alike?—What is carbon?—How are carbon compounds useful?—Why is carbon so special?—Fun facts about carbon.
    ISBN 0-516-22828-5 (lib. bdg.)   0-516-27848-7 (pbk.)
    1. Carbon—Juvenile literature. [1. Carbon.] I. Title. II. Series.
QD181.C1T63 2004
546'.681—dc22   2003016209

1 2 3 4 5 6 7 8 9 10 R 13 12 11 10 09 08 07 06 05 04

Contents

Although these two students are opposite in some ways, they still have something in common.

Can Opposites Be Alike?

Do you have two friends who are opposite from one another in some ways? For example, one friend may be a girl, while the other is a boy. One friend may be tall, while the other is short. One friend may have long hair, while the other may have short hair. Even though your friends may be opposite in some ways, they still may have things in common. Both of your friends, for example, may say that science is their favorite subject in school.

If you look closely enough, you may find that many opposites do have something in common. One example can be seen when comparing graphite and diamond. Graphite is commonly called pencil lead. Graphite is black and very soft, making it useful

Despite their differences, both graphite and diamond are made of carbon.

for writing on paper. Graphite is also used to lubricate, or grease, machine parts, and it conducts electricity well.

Diamond is very different from graphite. Diamond is clear and hard. In fact, diamond is the hardest substance known, making it useful for cutting and drilling through rocks. Unlike graphite, diamond does not conduct electricity well. Even though they are opposite in other ways, too, graphite and diamond have something in common. They are both made of carbon.

What Is Carbon?

Carbon is an element. An **element** is the building block of **matter**. Matter is the stuff or material that makes up everything in the universe. This book, the chair you are sitting on, and even your body, are made of matter.

There are millions of different kinds of matter. However, there are just a few more than one hundred different elements. How can so many different kinds of matter be made up of so few elements? Think about the English language. Just twenty-six letters can be arranged to make up all the words in the language. Likewise, approximately one hundred elements can be

Carbon is the sixth most abundant element in the universe.

combined in different ways to make up all the kinds of matter in the universe.

Every element has a name and a symbol. The symbol for carbon is C, the first letter in its name. The word "carbon" comes from the word *carbo,* which is Latin for charcoal. Charcoal is made by heating wood to very high temperatures under airtight conditions. When someone lights charcoal in a barbecue grill, he or she is burning carbon. Charcoal is mostly carbon with small amounts of other substances

in it. Carbon has been known since ancient times as the black soot that forms when wood or coal burns. Like charcoal, coal is mostly carbon.

Graphite, diamond, charcoal, soot, and coal are some of the forms in which you can find carbon as an element in nature. However, carbon can also combine with other elements to make compounds. A **compound** is a substance that is made from the combination of two or more different elements. Compounds containing carbon have a wide variety of uses.

How Are Carbon Compounds Useful?

Oxygen is one element that combines with carbon to form compounds. Carbon dioxide is probably the best known compound made of carbon and oxygen. Animals, including humans, make carbon dioxide inside their bodies during a process called respiration. **Respiration** is the process living things use to get energy from the foods they eat. Respiration uses oxygen and makes carbon dioxide as a waste product. Animals get rid of the carbon dioxide they make by breathing it out.

Although carbon dioxide is not useful to animals, plants need it to survive. Plants use carbon dioxide in

carbon dioxide

Animals, such as cows, breathe out the carbon dioxide made during respiration.

carbon dioxide

Plants, such as grasses, take in carbon dioxide to use during photosynthesis.

a process called photosynthesis. **Photosynthesis** is the process plants use to make food. Plants use the carbon dioxide they take in to make this food.

Animals depend on plants for their food. When animals eat plants, they break down the food in plants to use in respiration. The carbon that was in the plants is made into carbon dioxide. This carbon dioxide is released by animals

Carbon Cycle

carbon dioxide

carbon dioxide

Carbon is constantly being recycled in nature.

during respiration. The amount of carbon dioxide released by respiration is a large amount. Humans release about eight billion tons of carbon dioxide into the air each year.

Much of this carbon dioxide is then used by plants. As a result, carbon is being exchanged constantly between animals and plants. This exchange is part of the carbon cycle. The **carbon cycle** is nature's way of recycling carbon.

Making Carbon Dioxide

Respiration is not the only way to make carbon dioxide. You can also make carbon dioxide by mixing a few products you probably have at home. Add 1 tablespoon of baking soda and 1 tablespoon of laundry detergent or liquid hand soap to a tall drinking glass. Tilt the glass and slowly pour 1/2 cup of water down the side of the glass to avoid making soap bubbles. Add a few drops of food coloring.

Use a spoon to stir the contents of the glass gently.

Place the glass in a sink. Quickly pour 1/4 cup of vinegar into the glass. Watch what happens. The contents will foam up and over the sides of the glass. The foam is made up of tiny carbon dioxide gas bubbles that are produced by the baking soda and vinegar. The carbon dioxide causes even more bubbles to form in the soap. The food coloring just adds color.

For millions of years, the carbon cycle has been in balance. In other words, all the carbon dioxide released into the air by animals has been taken in and used by plants. Recently, however, more carbon dioxide than can be used by plants is being released into the air. Most of this extra carbon dioxide comes from the burning of fuels, such as coal and gasoline, that contain carbon.

The exhaust from motor vehicles created by burning gasoline releases carbon dioxide into the air.

Carbon dioxide is called a "greenhouse gas" because it traps the sun's heat like a greenhouse does.

Carbon dioxide that is not used by plants rises into the air, where it collects above Earth. Along with some other gases, carbon dioxide builds up and causes Earth's temper-ature to get slightly warmer over time. Scientists are not sure how this warming will affect weather patterns in the future. However, scientists are concerned because even a slight warming can have serious effects.

Why Is Carbon So Special?

Unlike most other elements, carbon can combine with itself. Hundreds of carbon particles can join together to form compounds. Carbon also can combine easily with one, two, three, or even four other elements. As a result, carbon forms more kinds of

Carbon compounds make up our bodies, the foods we eat, and the clothes we wear.

compounds than any other element does. These carbon compounds are found in all living things, in the foods we eat, in the clothes we wear, and in the products we use every day.

Meats are high in protein, potatoes are high in carbohydrate, and ice cream is high in fat.

With some exceptions, compounds that contain carbon are called **organic compounds**.

Organic compounds that are found in living things include proteins, carbohydrates, and fats. Proteins are used to help build the structure of a living thing, especially skin, muscles, and hair. Carbohydrates are used to supply energy. Fats are used for building parts of the body and are also stored in case they are needed to be burned to supply energy. Animals get the organic compounds they need from the foods they eat.

Breaking Down Carbohydrates

Soft drinks contain sugars, which are carbohydrates. Our bodies use sugar as a source of energy. When sugars are broken down through respiration, carbon dioxide is produced. You can trap the carbon dioxide that is made and use it to blow up a balloon.

Open a bottle of soda and allow it to go flat overnight. The next day, add 1 teaspoon (5 ml) of active dry yeast to the soda. Cap the bottle tightly and shake it. Remove the cap and stretch a balloon over the mouth of the bottle. Use a round, thin latex balloon and make sure it fits tightly over the bottle. Place the bottle in a warm area but not in direct sunlight, for several hours. The yeast will break down the sugars in the soda and make carbon dioxide gas that will slowly inflate the balloon.

Natural gas is another organic compound that contains carbon. Kerosene, gasoline, and home heating oil are mixtures of several organic compounds. All these compounds are made of only two elements—carbon and hydrogen.

If the element oxygen is present, these compounds can burn to provide heat and electricity for homes and energy to power automobiles and factories. Furnaces and engines must operate properly so that plenty of oxygen is made available for the burning process. If the furnace in a home is defective and does not provide enough oxygen, then a very poisonous substance is produced. This substance is called carbon monoxide. If carbon monoxide gets into the bloodstream, a person can die from a lack of oxygen.

Many homes have carbon
monoxide detectors.

Proteins, carbohydrates, fats, and natural gas are known as natural organic compounds because they are made in nature. Scientists have also made organic compounds in laboratories. These are known as synthetic organic compounds. A **synthetic compound** is one that is made in a laboratory or in some type of industrial plant. Synthetic compounds that contain carbon have become part of our daily lives. These

WNBA player Cynthia Cooper's uniform, sneakers, and the basketball she's dribbling, are all made from synthetic compounds that contain carbon.

compounds include plastics, fibers used to make some clothing, and adhesives.

Synthetic compounds are sometimes more useful than the natural compounds on which they are based. Rubber is an example. Natural rubber is produced by trees. This natural compound is made of two elements, carbon and hydrogen. Whenever natural rubber gets warm, it becomes very soft and gooey. As a result, natural rubber has few practical uses. For example, tires made of natural rubber would melt in warm weather.

In 1839, Charles Goodyear was experimenting with natural rubber. He had added another element to the soft rubber when he accidentally dropped some onto a hot stove. Goodyear noticed that the rubber did not melt, but instead got much stronger. The synthetic compound Goodyear made is called

Both the pain reliever tablets and the plastic container are made from synthetic carbon compounds.

vulcanized rubber. Vulcanized rubber is used to make tires, rain gear, rubber bands, and garden hoses. Today, we depend on hundreds of synthetic carbon compounds, such as vulcanized rubber, to make our lives healthier, safer, and more enjoyable.

Fun Facts About Carbon

- The largest diamond ever found weighed 3,106 carats, or almost 1.75 pounds (0.795 kilograms).

- A strange form of carbon called a buckyball was first discovered in stars billions of miles from Earth. Buckyballs are also found on Earth in such places as the soot that forms from a burning candle.

- The trees in 1 acre (0.4 hectares) of forest use 6 tons of carbon dioxide for photosynthesis each year.

- Carbon is used to make cast iron, wrought iron, steel, and stainless steel.

- Carbon is used to determine the age of some objects, such as seeds that were discovered among ancient ruins. These seeds were found to be ten thousand years old and grew when they were planted.

- Carbon black pigment is added to the rubber used to make tires. The carbon pigment protects the tires from drying out and becoming brittle from the sunlight.

To Find Out More

If you would like to learn more about carbon, check out these additional resources.

 **Books**

Blashfield, Jean F. **Carbon (Sparks of Life: Chemical Elements that Make Life Possible.)** TX: Raintree/ Steck-Vaughn, 1998.

Sparrow, Giles. **Carbon.** NY: Marshall Cavendish, 1999.

Uehling, Mark D. **The Story of Carbon.** CT: Franklin Watts, 1995.

Organizations and Online Sites

American Museum of Natural History
Central Park West at
79th Street
New York, NY 10024-5192
*www.amnh.org/exhibitions/
diamonds/carbon.html*

Learn how carbon that came from the stars forms diamonds deep inside Earth. This site also contains information on how diamonds come to the surface and where they are found. Read about how some diamonds contain elements other than carbon and how these elements affect a diamond's quality.

Carbon for Kids
www.icbe.com/carbonforkids

This site explores the process through which greenhouse gases promote global warming. Some interesting facts about carbon dioxide are also provided, including the fact that each person in the United States produces 20 tons of carbon dioxide every year.

The Carbon Cycle
*www.epa.gov/
globalwarming/kids/
carbon_cycle_version2html*

Watch a short movie that shows how carbon is recycled on land and in water. Learn how the burning and the cutting down of forests are affecting the carbon cycle.

Carbon Monoxide
*http://crh.noaa.gov/mkx/
owlie/monoxide.htm*

This site provides safety tips to follow at home to prevent carbon monoxide poisoning.

Discovery Science Center
*www.discoverycube.org/
kids/exp0.htm*

Perform an experiment to make a fire extinguisher that uses carbon dioxide to put out a fire.

Important Words

carbon cycle process by which carbon is recycled in nature

compound substance formed from the combination of two or more different elements

element building block of matter

matter material that makes up everything in the universe

organic compound compound that contains carbon, with some exceptions such as carbon dioxide

photosynthesis process plants use to produce foods

respiration process living things use to obtain energy from the foods they eat

synthetic compound compound made in a laboratory or in an industrial plant

Index

Meet the Author

Salvatore Tocci is a science writer who lives in East Hampton, New York with his wife Patti. He was a high school biology and chemistry teacher for almost thirty years. His books include a high school chemistry textbook and an elementary school book series that encourages students to perform experiments to learn about science. The most impressive diamonds he has seen are those in the Crown Jewels of the British royal family that are on display in the Tower of London.